Copyright © 2018 by Sarah J. Cadore
All rights reserved.

VMH Vikki M. Hankins™ Publishing
www.vmhpublishing.com

Without limiting the rights under copyright reserved above, no part of this publication may be reproduced, stored in or introduced into a retrieval system, or transmitted, in any form or by any means.

Published in the United States by VMH Publishing.

Hardback ISBN: 978-1-947928-03-9

Paperback ISBN: 978-1-947928-16-9

10 9 8 7 6 5 4 3 2 1

Book Cover Design: Vikki Jones

Interior Layout: VMH Publishing

Interior Images Courtesy Unsplash, Pixabay

Printed in the United States of America.

Publisher's Note:
The publisher is not responsible for the content of this book nor websites, or social media pages (or their content) that are not owned by the publisher.

You Don't Have To Be Old To Be Wise

Dedication

To my sons, Austin and Joshua, and to all my nieces, nephews, and cousins who have not had the opportunity to experience the wisdom of their beloved great-grandparents, Ellick and Elmitta. It is my hope that by reading these aphorisms they will at least get a feel for what it was like to grow up among such great souls who sought to empower the younger generation and present a lasting and positive effect on every life they came in contact with.

Acknowledgments

As a child growing up on the island of Grenada, I often marveled at the many statements of truths the older generation, in particular my grandparents, would speak, not only to me, my siblings, cousins, aunts and uncles, but to all those who anxiously sought their advice, or even to those who did not. What I did not know or understood at the time was that they were attempting to impress upon us the immeasurable wisdom they had acquired through their own journeys of life. Such impressions were not intended to prove to us how wise they were; instead, they were geared to positively influence our attitudes, beliefs, actions, and our perceptions. Those truths were food for thoughts; the older generation wanted us to be critical thinkers. They wanted us to thrive and not just exist.

The aphorisms they spoke continuously included sayings like:

- *Do not trouble "trouble" if you don't want "trouble" to trouble you.*
- *Unless your wish is to be bitten, leave sleeping dogs lie.*
- *Play with puppies and get bitten by their flees.*
- *Empty vessels are the noisiest.*
- *Work with what God gives you.*
- *Don't do to others what you would not want them do to you.*
- *Live today in anticipation of what you would like your life to be tomorrow.*
- *Waste not, and you will want for nothing.*
- *Save a little today for when it rains tomorrow.*
- *One bird in your hand is worth many birds in the bushes.*
- *Don't jump unless you know what you are jumping into.*
- *Even the darkest cloud has a silver lining.*
- *Spare not the rod and ruin the child.*
- *Life is like a bed of roses, you get the beauty and you get the spoil.*
- *Don't bite the hand that puts food in your stomach.*
- *An ounce of prevention is better than a whole pound of cure.*
- *Every dog has his day; today is yours, tomorrow might be mine.*
- *The evil that men do, leave that to them; their evil today will affect their tomorrow.*
- *A stitch in time saves nine.*
- *The early bird catches the worm.*
- *Strike the iron while it's hot.*

- *The grass is not always greener on the other side.*
- *Don't take medicine for other people's fever.*
- *Make hay while the sun shines.*
- *Unjust bread can never be digested.*
- *The faintest of ink is the best of memory.*
- *The ones you love are not always the ones who will love you.*
- *People who live in glass houses should not throw stones.*
- *A wise man's answer to a fool's argument is yes.*
- *Don't see chicken shit and call it eggs.*
- *Give a man a fish and he becomes your problem; teach him how to fish and he will solve many problems*
- *Depend not on the cover of a book to tell the whole story.*

My grandfather believed so strongly in statements of truths that he wrote on his fishing boat "GIVE TO GET." Other sayings of truths he believed in strongly and verbalized regularly, especially to his children and grandchildren were, "foolish is the man who never left, nor traveled away from the place of his birth," and "he who laughs last, laughs the best."

Of these truths, we would often laugh and say, "There they go again."

How naïve could we have been? Like so many young adults today, we thought we knew it all. We were unaware that they, in their simple, yet subtle ways, were preparing us for life's challenges; the ups and the downs, the good, the bad, and the ugly.

I know now that they were speaking life's truths. Most of that generation, including my grandparents, are no longer with us, but the wisdom they impressed upon those of us who listened have today become the lifeline that keeps us anchored in the ebbs and flows of our life's journey.

*****

"The ones you love are not always the ones who will love you." I was specifically reminded of this truth when I heard the story of a family who actually lived it.

There were two sisters, Jane and Jacinta. Jane had two sons: Leo and Derik, while Jacinta had an only son: Jude. Both sisters adored each other and loved their nephews unconditionally. Nothing was too difficult to do for any of the boys. Jane and Jacinta treated them as if they were brothers.

Unfortunately, Jacinta was involved in a catastrophic automobile accident which resulted in her demise. Jude was left under the guardianship of Jane since she was his only known next of kin. Jude never knew his father. As rumor had it, Jude's father was a young Marine who was shipped out to sea before Jude was born. A few months after his deployment, the Marine Corp reported him missing in action. Sadly, Jude was also estranged from the family on his father's side, who for untold reasons, were never introduced to Jude.

Although the sisters were inseparable when Jacinta was alive, Jane's attitude completely changed toward Jude soon after he became her ward. Jude was the same age as Jane's youngest son, Derik. They were also in the same grade, but Jude was and continued to be an honor roll student, who often made the Dean's list. Adversely, Derik was an average student who had never been on the honor roll or the Dean's List. This was always known to Jane; nevertheless, upon becoming Jude's guardian, and receiving his report card from school, she became consumed with jealousy. Instead of encouraging her grieving nephew to be the best that he could be, she chose to give him the Cinderella treatment.

Jane did everything possible for Jude to miss school or arrive late to his classes, and she constantly criticized his every move. She called him stupid and blamed him for everything that went wrong. Nothing he did pleased her. He was even subjected to capital punishment from time to time. He was the family's dishwasher, yard boy, messenger, janitor, and even their tutor. Many nights he was forced to go to bed without dinner because he might have been tardy in completing chores. While his cousins slept comfortably upstairs on their well made beds, Jude shared a cot in the cold and musty basement with their black, aging, husky dog: Paw. Adding insult to injury, Jane housed a vacant guestroom with his mother's seven-piece queen sized, mahogany bedroom set inside.

Jude did not allow his circumstance to change his well mannered attitude; neither did he allow it to put a damper on his dream of becoming a physician. He endured the hardship and while his cousins were sleeping on their cozy beds, in their well lit, heated bedrooms,

Jude stayed awake at nights, studying by the light of a kerosene lamp which his grandmother willed to his mother. He adhered to his aunt's strict instruction to turn off the electric light in the basement no later than 9:00 p.m.

Jude's hard work and perseverance resulted in him winning a scholarship to a prestigious university. He graduated cum laude and was accepted into medical school at that very same university where he completed his undergraduate degree. His continued diligence, hard work, and commitment to excellence again led him to graduate at the top of his class.

Over the years Jude's exceptional credentials, achievements, and contribution to cardiovascular medicine resulted in him becoming internationally known as one of the best in his field.

Meanwhile, Leo and Derik were provided an extremely privileged existence. They wanted for nothing; they attended the best universities they were able to gain acceptance to, with Jane financing their way throughout.

Jane's oldest son Leo went on to graduate school where he earned a master's degree in engineering, married, and then relocated to the city where his wife's parents lived. Derik, on the other hand, obtained a bachelor's degree, got married, and moved into his mother's house with his wife and two children.

Years later, Jane had a stroke and was hospitalized. Her left side was paralyzed and despite undergoing intense therapy, she continued to experience limited mobility in her left arm and leg.

Puzzled by her slow recovery, Jane's physicians conducted a barrage of tests which showed no physical impediment to a more robust recovery. With that diagnosis, they concluded that it was in Jane's best interest to recuperate in a familiar setting, most likely her home. They contended that such an environment would create for Jane, the emotional motivation she needed to attain a full and speedy recovery.

Derik accepted the diagnosis, but vehemently rejected the physicians' recommendation. He conveyed to them that he had no doubt that they were correct in their assessment of her condition. Nevertheless, he was not willing to have his sick mother disrupt or place any undue burden on his wife and children by having her return home before she was fully recovered.

"Under no condition will I put my wife and children through this ordeal," he argued. "I will never subject them to such stress, so find another solution or leave mother where she is."

He was adamant about his decision and no argument could change it. Even when Leo tried to shame him for taking his mother's home right from under her, he exhibited no remorse.

Leo agreed with the physicians' recommendation but continued to insist that Jane should be placed with Derik and his family since the house in which they reside belongs to her. He could not believe nor understand why Derik was willing to keep his mother out of her own home. After several heated arguments between Leo and Derik, Leo gave in and decided to let Derik have his way, nevertheless, he too remained unyielding. He would not shoulder the burden of having Jane move in with him and his family.

With Jane's physicians insistence that her recovery would be impeded by the environment in which she currently resides, Leo and Derik reached an agreement to have their mother transferred to a government-run rehabilitation center where there were patients with like conditions.

Jude abstained from the decision making process and the arguments between the brothers, but after they made the decision to move Jane to a government-run facility to be cared for by complete strangers, he stepped in and stopped the transfer. With the consent of Leo and Derik, he petitioned the hospital and Jane's physicians' to release Jane into his care. He moved Jane into his home with the equipment she needed for her rehabilitation therapy, and hired an in-home registered nurse to take care of Jane's medical needs. Jude also hired a physical therapist to help Jane work on her motor skills and offered his cousins an open invitation to visit Jane as often as they saw fit.

Without hesitation, Jude's wife and children welcomed his decision to care for the person who provided him a roof over his head when it counted, despite the hardship he endured while living under that roof. With gratitude, they willingly assisted with Jane's rehabilitation.

Shortly thereafter, Jane recovered and continued to reside in the home of Jude, her nephew. For her convenience, he converted the west wing of his home to an in-law suite and invited Jane to live there as long as she so desired.

Later, when asked why they refused to have Jane convalesce with them and their family, both Leo and Derik communicated that their love for their mother could not be unconditional. They had no doubt that Jane loved them but after becoming parents themselves, they found it difficult to understand how any parent could treat a child the way their mother treated Jude. They were both haunted by that realization and as a result could not trust their mother's love completely. They went on to say that it was hard not to imagine her physically and emotionally abusing their children as she did Jude, should she decide to favor some over the others.

Neither Leo nor Derik was willing to take that chance. They would not be burdened by someone they could not completely love or trust. Neither could they ask their family to bear such a burden. Additionally, Derik argued that his mother would have had to will the house to him sooner or later, so leaving it sooner was not a problem for him.

When asked why he invited his aunt Jane to live with him and his family in spite of the way she had treated him, Jude's response was that he had always loved his aunt for who she was and not for whom she had become. He went on to say that if he had been allowed the same privileges as did his cousins, things might not have worked out for him the way they did. He might have become complacent and relinquished his childhood dream of becoming a physician, and with a smile, he added, "I might have thrown diligence out the window!"

In retrospect, Jude believed that he was made stronger and more resilient because of his aunt's harsh treatment of him, and for that, he thanked her. What she thought would have weakened him, made him stronger and more focused on who he wanted to become. Jude also contended that through his experience, he learned what not to do to others, and as his profession dictates, "do no harm." Jude encouraged his children to always *do onto others as they would have others do onto them.*

As for Jane, all she said about her behavior toward Jude was that she was truly ashamed of her actions, and after asking Jude for his forgiveness, and receiving it, she vowed never to again discuss that period in her life. Nonetheless, Jane grieved in silence. She was dumbfounded by the harshness of her children's actions toward her; she could not understand why the love she gave was not reciprocated by those she gave it too.

*****

How many of our young adults would be able to undergo the suffering and the hardship that Jude endured, yet, go on to achieve what he had achieved? Are we preparing them to thrive through the storms of life, or are we just teaching them how to survive?

We are surely not able to shield them from the Janes' of this world, but it is our responsibility to provide for them a foundation on which to build upon, and the necessary tools needed for such occurrences as in the case of Jude. Such tools should be geared to making our young adults more resilient, purposeful, bold, diligent, and ready to persevere and prevail in spite of the circumstances in which they may find themselves.

Like our grandparents and the generation before us who strove to enlighten and empower us, the onus now falls upon us to take up the reins and show our young adults not only how to exist in a world designed to beat them down, but give them the tools they need to blossom in such a world. It is now up to us to feed them 'food for thought,' and encourage them to think in critical ways that would cause them to thrive instead of survive and to live instead of merely exist.

With this premise in mind, I share my truths hoping that they will in some way serve as beacons, guiding our young adults and adults alike as they journey through life's pathways, experiencing the ups and the downs, the good, the bad, and the ugly on their way to their greatest achievements in life.

STORMS OF LIFE ARE EQUALLY OPPORTUNISTIC; THEY ARE RESPECTERS OF NO ONE

Success comes to those who are not afraid to persevere through the storms of life.

He who perseveres in spite of turmoil will reap great rewards.

Every problem is an opportunity waiting to take flight; it is up to you to steer it in the right direction.

He who lived his life sheltered from the experiences of adversity had gained no knowledge of what it really meant to be alive.

Out of chaos and suffering come strength; for that which didn't kill you will make you a whole lot stronger.

Our true purpose is born through the pain and suffering we are tough enough to endure.

Be not anxious about impending obstacles, for unlike birth pain they arrive unexpectedly, so with every obstacle you conquer, count your blessings and keep moving.

Running away from what seems difficult will leave you unequipped to make it through the storms of life; face your demons and become stronger and better equipped to bear the weight that life may throw upon you.

When challenged by our experiences, the way we respond will determine whether we thrive or just survive, or whether we sink or float. Respond with clarity of mind.

Persevere and build character in life's battle. You may be knocked down, beaten, and bruised, but not giving up makes you resilient and much more prepared for the war.

Boast not about the good life until you face adversity, especially the trials you never saw coming. Prideful boasters seldom recover.

Your journey may be long and hard, but every stride taken with an eye to the finish line brings you closer to your destination. Imagine yourself at the end of the race and exhale with jubilation.

You are oblivious of your strength until you are faced with a problem and your instinct takes over. Believe in yourself, you can do more than you think possible; just imagine.

Ignore those who criticize for the sake of criticizing, but be receptive to constructive criticism for that might be all you need to move you from a life of mediocrity to one of superiority.

Not every conversation deserves a loquacious participant; more knowledge is gained by listening than by talking. An exceptional listener increases in wisdom and often times helps mend broken hearts.

"If" is irreversible and the hardest word in the dictionary. It is the epitome of regrets. Let not "if" become your life's mantra (*What if, if I had known, if I had done this or that.. if, if, if*).

If you keep thinking about the "what if's", you will never see the "what will be."

Be not afraid to start something new though it might be the hardest thing to do. Through all the pain and heartache just remember, it is not where you start, it is where you finish; all it takes is a step in the right direction.

A MAN CANNOT RUN FOREVER, NEITHER CAN HE HIDE FROM WHAT IS TO COME

Hide not from minute challenges for they will grow and catch up with you in ways you will not be able to withstand.

Deal now with every challenge as it comes and in so doing, you will learn enough and know enough to handle the majors when and if they do appear.

The man who plans his course has a better chance of escape than the man who decides to wing it.

Be not like the man who waits until he is directly affected by wrong doings before he becomes angry enough to take a stand. By then, it may be too late. A wise man helps put out his neighbor's fire before it creeps onto his property.

It's easy to blame past generations for our inability to change while refusing to alter our attitudes. Stop hiding behind the so called generational curse syndrome or the change within us that is struggling to escape will never be released. Chart your own individual course and leave the generational curse syndrome where it belongs, in the past.

Be careful what you do to others, for in all likelihood it will come back to you. Do good or do nothing; it is better to have nothing come back to you than it is to have a load of hot ash heaped upon your head.

Cherish the memories of the past but leave space in your heart big enough for new memories as your life's journey continues.

An optimistic and responsible man laughs at his mistakes, learns from his mistakes, and blames no one for his mistakes.

TIME AND TIDE WAIT FOR NO MAN
Geoffrey Chaucer

He who procrastinates will soon realize that his body will not wait for him, neither will his mind, and as for time, it will just keep on ticking.

Time wasted can never be regained nor can it be bought; use it prudently without being programmed by the clock.

Today may not be your day, but remember that there are three hundred and sixty-five days in a calendar year and three hundred and sixty-six days in each leap year. Live to try again another day.

You can't repeat your yesterday, but you can make your tomorrow better by using the experiences of your yesterday.

Live life with a purpose, for it is uncertain and can end in an instant. Do whatever you are capable of doing today for there may never be a tomorrow.

Busy not yourself worrying about your tomorrow for you will miss the radiance of your today.

Take a good look at where you are at this very moment in time, chances are, you may never see yourself there again.

After the shock wears out, spend less time talking about what man had done to you and more time working on your comeback. Give not your energy to those who hurt you by dwelling on what they have done to you; let your success tell them who and what you really are.

Time lost in anger could be better spent in creativity, which in the long run could lead to something bigger and more significant than what caused you to be angry in the first place.

Time is a lucrative commodity, invest it wisely.

Wait not until your time expires before realizing how valuable it is. There is much to create in space and in time, over which you have no control. You can spend time creating but you cannot create time.

Say what's in your heart to those you love today, for you may never get another chance to say it; act today, tomorrow is a gamble.

Time can never be reversed.

The difference in value between time and money is that if lost, you can get more money, but you can't get more time. In a nutshell, time is more valuable than money.

The most valuable time is the time one spends improving one's self and or improving someone else.

FEAR: THE GREATEST DETERRENT TO ONE'S DESTINY

If you are afraid of the unknown, how will you know exactly what in the unknown you are afraid of? Take a chance.

Deal with your fears, or whatever scares you will become your reality.

The strength of a bully lies in what he perceives to be the weakness of his victim; he fearfully retreats when the one he perceives to be timid stands his ground. Don't allow fear to turn you into a victim.

Hide not behind excuses; use instead the adrenalin stimulated by your fear as a catalyst to propel you towards progress rather than flight; it is only a matter of time before one runs out of excuses.

Every question thought of and feared to ask robs us of the knowledge we might otherwise obtain.

When challenged by fear, we can either conquer it by facing it head on or be conquered by it through our inaction.

Fear hinders those who easily succumb rather than push forward no matter the circumstance.

If David allowed fear to deter him, Goliath might still be alive.

A courageous man does not overcome fear by eliminating it; he overcomes fear by learning to persevere through it.

The mistake you are afraid of making may be the mistake that leads to your invention. Let not fear of failure paralyze the creativity in you.

Be not afraid of failure, it is not a death sentence; rather, it is the fetus of an enduring man. With every miscarriage, keep on trying, soon success will be born.

Embark not on a journey if you fear failure from the start. To be successful, you must envision success at the finish line, not the difficulties you will encounter on your way there.

A man who had neither failed, nor feared, lived a life of nothing: no dreams, no goals, no love, no taking chances; he cowardly existed.

The greatest inventors in the world succeeded because they persevered in the face of fear and never stopped trying no matter how many times they failed.

If you permit fear to keep you from getting out of your comfort zone, you will never get out of your comfort zone.

Develop not a defeatist attitude; it is better to try and fail than it is to fail to try. Where there is no action, hope dies, leaving you to wonder if you would have succeeded had you really tried.

Forfeit not the good you might achieve by failing to endeavor.

Be not discouraged by failure, embrace it and use it as an opportunity to grow; it could become your greatest motivator.

TODAY'S LIVING IS A DIRECT CONSEQUENCE OF YESTERDAY'S CHOICES

Whatever becomes of your tomorrow is determined by choices you make today; choose wisely.

Nothing done in the absence of the heart is worth doing. Whatever you choose to do, do it passionately and with a willing mind; give it all you've got.

Not every fight deserves an active participant; your chosen fights should be purposeful, win or lose.

The ugly whispers of the crowd propel its recipient to greatness when he or she chooses not to become victimized by gossips that are meant to penetrate the psyche. Turn off the external noise and strive to cultivate the gifts within you.

The appeaser is loved by everyone until he becomes his own man and chooses to stand for something.

Habits are hard to form, but once they take root, they become difficult to eradicate. Be careful what habits you choose to form.

To change your life and circumstances, you must first choose to renew your mind and envision the change you wish to become.

When surrounded by wrong doers, wrong doing becomes part of you; guard your future and choose carefully the company you keep. The influence of others could determine your life's final destination. Be the solitary apple that falls out of the bunch before becoming infested by that one bad apple.

Spontaneity may be regarded as bravery, but it is also a vehicle for regrets; think before you act and save yourself from a whole heap of turmoil.

A good listener increases in wisdom while a talkative man divulges irretrievable information that was never meant for the consumption of others. Talk not until you have nothing else to say, save something for another day.

No matter where you are planted in life, you will blossom if only you will choose to find, groom, and develop that untapped potential within you.

Inspiration is all around you, open your mind, your eyes, and your heart and you will find it.

There is no shortness of bad in this world, but if you choose to see the good in everyone and in every situation, you will most likely find it, and that in itself will enhance the good in you.

Of the many options that will be placed before you during your journey of life, let failure not be one of them.

UNREACHABLE DREAMS ARE THE ONES WE FAIL TO DREAM

Impose no limitations on your dreams, for nothing is impossible; however, be mindful that not all that is possible is right.

We all have a destiny to fulfill as long as we are alive and breathing, but that destiny becomes futile the moment we stop dreaming.

Let not your dreams fall by the wayside; pursue them despite the naysayers and the fears which are impediments to the weak at heart. Fight for your dreams and the impediments will gradually disappear.

Dreams are unreachable only when you stop dreaming or when you fail to chase them.

We all have the power within us to fulfill our God-given destiny; the question is do we have the strength and the determination to dig deep enough to find that power when things are not going the way we planned? Plans can be adjusted, persevere against all odds and what once seemed impossible will become real.

It is difficult to execute the fulfillment of one's destiny in the absence of a vision and the inflexibility of a plan.

Every dream has a destination, but it is up to you to guide it along its pathway no matter how treacherous the terrain might become.

The onus is yours to cultivate whatever lies within you; work on your talent or it will die an unwilling death right before your very eyes.

Limit not your destiny by validating other people's opinion of you; what you think of yourself is really what matters. No one knows you like you do.

If you rely on external forces to determine your future, like a top you will find yourself spinning around and around but going nowhere.

Be not like anybody else, bypass mediocrity and set your sights toward unending possibilities to become the best you, you can become.

Anyone who is deterred by the ignorance of others has yet to attain the gift of self awareness. Know yourself; let no one define who you are.

Break out of mediocrity for you have the power within to be greater and to do better than you can ever imagine.

A man without a dream is synonymous to a chicken without a head; he keeps on flopping in every direction with no set destination.

Until you find your real life's purpose, your true potential will remain stifled within you and will never be realized.

WE ARE RESPONSIBLE FOR WHATEVER WE BECOME

Well directed energy supersedes drowning one's self in sorrow or wallowing in self-pity.

Being independent does not mean living in and of ones self, no man is an island.

It is said that to every action there is a reaction, but every reaction does not have to be an action.

Keep taking the high road and soon those who persecute you will follow the tracks which you have left behind.

Be cautious of the man who always complains to you about others, he is likewise complaining to others about you.

If all you do is follow the crowd, you will never find your own way.

If you only do what everyone else is doing, the potential that lies within you will never be realized.

A greedy man will never be satisfied until his thirst for more becomes his Albatross.

A man who agrees with everything stands for nothing. He is like a big ship in a storm waiting to be turned by a small rudder, in whatever direction the pilot desires.

Know yourself in order to be yourself.

Make learning a continuous and never ending process for in each and every one of us lies room for improvement.

Know who you are or you will become anything anyone wants you to be.

Revenge can be overrated; don't get mad, succeed.

It's hard to let go of the wrong that's done to you; however, it is dangerous to let it fester within, for dwelling on the "has been" will keep you from achieving the "what will be." Learn to forgive.

If you keep looking into the rearview mirror, you will miss the splendor of what lies ahead of you.

Envy not a man's possession for you know not what he did to possess it.

The words of a drunken man should be taken seriously; he speaks from his heart what he is thinking, but is too afraid to say with sobriety.

Get rid of the little boy who always cries wolf syndrome, or the cries over the real wolf will go unheard.

If you complain about everything, no one will hear you when it really matters.

Telling a lie over and over does not make it true; you may even start believing those lies if you tell them long enough, and in so doing you may soon find yourself living a false reality. What is actual truth will become to you a conspiracy. This however, becomes detrimental when your followers start to naively believe your lies without doing due diligence to seek out truth from fiction.

Fraternize not with temptation, nor put in front of you what does not belong in you; being strong-willed is not the bedrock of human nature.

Guard the thoughts that occupy your mind, for a man becomes what he thinks. If he thinks negatively, he gets negative results; likewise, positive thinking brings forth positive results.

Don't just live life, love it. Exert passion in all that you do and prove yourself to no one but you. Know what's in you, beneath you, around you, and greater than you; be the author of your own story.

STRONG LEADERS ACCEPT CHANGE WITHOUT SACRIFICING VALUES, BELIEFS, AND THE RULE OF LAW

A true leader focuses not only on the greatness he can achieve, but on what he can do to enrich others. He has the power to unlock great potential both within himself and in those he help along the way.

As we encourage others to find their true potential, we too will find within ourselves ideals we never thought we possessed.

Every man can be your teacher; it all depends on what you are willing to learn.

No man wants to be a loser, but losing once in a while keeps him grounded and makes winning that much sweeter.

Though you may have struggled to be the first to get to the top, don't hesitate to leave a light burning to illuminate the way for those who come after you. They may even go ahead of you, but you will be remembered and cherished for being the trailblazer.

If you do not know where you came from, you will never know where you are going, nor will you know when you get there.

A life well lived is not measured by how much you achieved, but by how much you gave and how many lives you enriched throughout your journey.

An arrogant man in the position of leadership is not to be trusted; in his mind he knows everything and will learn nothing. He will take you to war without counting the cost, his reflexes are faster than his thoughts, and his heart is as barren as the desert.

Look into the heart of an arrogantly braggadocios leader and you will see a hole as big as his ego waiting to be filled by something he craves but can never have: respect.

To become a "somebody," you must first learn how to be a "nobody."

A leader is not just someone in charge applying techniques and tactics to solve problems; we are all leaders in our own rights, leading not always in obvious or dramatic ways, but most often in subtle and incalculable ways.

A great leader engages in an ongoing process of self development while at the same time exploring ways to bring out the hidden leadership qualities in others. He knows how to be inclusive and how to embrace change in a diverse world that is constantly changing.

A good leader rather than complain about the problem or blame the originator of the problem, seeks solutions to the problem while envisioning the good that can be had from the occurrence of the problem.

There is no need to boast of how great you are, for by your deeds one will know your greatness; action speaks louder than words.

A GOOD RELATIONSHIP LASTS LONGER THAN A LIFETIME

A good relationship begins with you; love yourself before you can love others or expect others to love you.

An empty heart is a cesspool for despair, fill it with love and there will be joy.

A mother's love is the closest we can get to God's love. They love you unconditionally, no matter how far you stray.

The love and kindness you show to others may become the legacy you leave behind.

Be not afraid to give generously of yourself, it will come back to you a hundred fold.

Compromise not your joy, your peace of mind, or your values, for promotion and popularity, for that in the end, will only bring you misery.

A meaningful conversation and a whole lot of laughter are the surest cure for the weakest of hearts and minds.

Be careful who you bring into your life, for happiness begets happiness and joy begets joy. An unhappy man will only be happy if you too are unhappy.

If a relationship seems wrong at the onset, chances are, it is wrong; entrench not yourself deeper into that relationship with hopes that things will change. It is easier to walk away than it is to be pulled away.

Real friends lift you up when you struggle and pull you in when you stray. Like magnets, they stick to you through thick and thin and keep you on the straight and narrow path even through raging storms.

Ignore the negative labels that are placed upon you by others, for they can stick to you like leeches and never let go until your true potential is sapped away by the doubts they sow within you.

The respect you give to others is a reflection of the respect you have for yourself. You cannot give what you do not have, so respect yourself and you will have no problem respecting others, and they in turn will respect you.

He who makes important decisions in the midst of an emotional meltdown creates for himself an impetus for regrets that may last a lifetime.

Being popular is not analogous to being loved. The moment your magnetism hits a road block, those who flock to you will disappear, but during such a time you realize who your real friends are: those who stick around.

Grieve not over the so called friends you might lose along the way, this might be the best thing that ever happens to you.

DEGREES & HIGH IQ'S ARE NOT PREREQUISITES FOR FINANCIAL GAIN

Let not your circumstances define you; if you dislike the situation you are in, alter your mindset and create the circumstances you envision.

He, who develops a clearly defined goal for his future, has no reason to conform to what everyone else is doing; he has created a roadmap to his destination.

Forget not to redeposit at least ten percent of your earnings into the coffers of the Master who gave it to you in the first place, tithe.

In all that you do, let your money work for you. Pay yourself by investing or saving at least ten percent of whatever you earn; wealth is not what you spend, it is what you accumulate.

Becoming wealthy is not a short term process, among other things; invest today and enjoy the harvest tomorrow.

Working hard won't kill you, but working smart will ease the pain that working hard inflicts upon you.

Think right, sacrifice not your future by clinging to your past; that which you have lost is gone, concentrate on new beginnings and utilize your past experiences to minimize future mistakes.

Visualize clearly the person you wish to become and purge yourself from those who are incapable of cheering you on past the starting line.

Be a risk taker; great achievers are seldom found in their comfort zones.

Live within your means and hang not your bonnet where your hand can't reach.

Use what you have in anticipation of getting what you want; many great men started with nothing but vigor, ambition, and a strong dose of imagination.

To obtain sound investment advice, don't ask the baker, the butcher, or the candlestick maker, ask a financial advisor. Your financial health is important; treat it as you would a headache, cautiously seek the help of an expert.

He, who is not afraid to pursue personal development and consistent learning with carefully organized execution of knowledge, will create for himself a greater earning potential.

To succeed, find out what successful people are doing and learn to do it better without changing who you are. Simply become the best you, you can be.

Don't do what the crowd is doing, do what the winners are doing.

Before deciding to stand in line to purchase the name brand product, consider how short the line is where you can instead purchase a share of the company.

In life, what matters is not how much you have, but what you do with what you have; use it for good.

WITH FAITH EVERYTHING IS POSSIBLE AND NOTHING IS IMPOSSIBLE

Trust God even when you feel that all is lost, for in his arms you are carried even though you may not feel it.

Don't forget to sow, for as you sow, so shall you reap.

Master the art of giving, for as you give, so shall you receive.

Throughout your journey, set aside some quiet time each day, for it is written that the stillness of the heart stores up peace within.

Pray for those who hurt you, and be not afraid to offer a hand to all those in need.

Harbor not the burden of unforgiveness, for it will only weigh you down. Forgive those who hurt you and the burden you feel within will diminish.

Forgive others but don't forget to forgive yourself.

Nothing you embark upon will come to fruition until you believe that it will.

In all that you do, know that there is someone greater than you are. Be thankful.

With every blessing you receive, don't forget to bless others.

The pain you feel in your heart will subside when you truly believe that you were not brought this far to be left alone by the one who says he will never leave you nor forsake you.

Keep always in your heart Matthew 7:7. "Ask and it shall be given you; seek, and ye shall find; knock, and it shall be opened unto you." These promises are made to all who believe. Believe.

Of the numerous things my grandmother did, she loved telling stories and reciting poems to all the neighborhood children who gathered around at least once a month to listen to her fascinating, gripping, and sometimes scary zombie stories, all with a lesson to be learned. One of the poems she loved reciting was "Drive the Nail Aright Boy" taken from The Royal Reader series. I find it necessary to share this memorable and insightful poem as a lesson to be learned.

DRIVE THE NAIL ARIGHT BOY

Drive the nail aright, boy
Hit it on the head
Strike with all your might, boy,
While the iron's red.

When you have work to do, boy
Do it with your will
They who reach the top, boy,
First must climb the hill.

Standing at the foot, boy,
Looking at the sky,
How can you get up, boy,
If you never try?

Though you stumble oft, boy,
Never be downcast;
Try and try again, boy—
You will succeed at last.

Through all the peaks and the valleys, the good days and the bad days, the happy and the sad days, 'don't give up'.

The journey is a character builder but you will not know its value until you have reached your destination.

www.ingramcontent.com/pod-product-compliance
Lightning Source LLC
La Vergne TN
LVHW051203080426
835508LV00021B/2772